FINDING *the* SHAMAN

SPIRITUAL JOURNEY BACK TO TRUE SELF

DEBRA LEE HILLARY

AKA. Rainbow Medicine Women

BALBOA
PRESS

A DIVISION OF HAY HOUSE

Balboa Press books may be ordered through booksellers or by contacting:

Balboa Press
A Division of Hay House
1663 Liberty Drive
Bloomington, IN 47403
www.balboapress.com
1 (877) 407-4847

Because of the dynamic nature of the Internet, any web addresses or
links contained in this book may have changed since publication and
may no longer be valid. The views expressed in this work are solely those
of the author and do not necessarily reflect the views of the publisher,
and the publisher hereby disclaims any responsibility for them.

The author of this book does not dispense medical advice or prescribe the use
of any technique as a form of treatment for physical, emotional, or medical
problems without the advice of a physician, either directly or indirectly. The
intent of the author is only to offer information of a general nature to help
you in your quest for emotional and spiritual well-being. In the event you use
any of the information in this book for yourself, which is your constitutional
right, the author and the publisher assume no responsibility for your actions.

Any people depicted in stock imagery provided by Thinkstock are
models, and such images are being used for illustrative purposes only.
Certain stock imagery © Thinkstock.

Print information available on the last page.

ISBN: 978-1-5043-6126-2 (sc)
ISBN: 978-1-5043-6125-5 (e)

Library of Congress Control Number: 2016910942

Balboa Press rev. date: 09/07/2016

I dedicate this book to my family and acknowledge my ancestors.

"All My Relations" Rainbow x

TABLE OF CONTENTS

Foreword ix

Preface...xi

Chapter 1 * In the Beginning-Training Ground 1

Chapter 2 * Full Connection to Disconnection 7

Chapter 3 * Fresh Start in the Gatineau Hills......................... 13

Chapter 4 * Relocation to the West (Returning Home) 17

Chapter 5 * Teachers Appear 23

Chapter 6 * Meeting My Life mate 30

Chapter 7 * Balancing Act..40

Chapter 8 * Wide Awake 47

Chapter 9 * Wisdom Teachings...52

Chapter 10 * With Much Gratitude 56

About the Author 65

FOREWORD

Through ceremony and storytelling, shamans in different cultures all over the world have brought healing to their communities. Here on the west coast of Canada, our First Nations elders teach ancient wisdom passed on in the oral tradition, rarely written down. The connection to the land and the water, the earth and the universe, is inherent in all the teachings. As well, our connection to each other, to the creatures roaming, flying and swimming, and to all plant life is clear. In harming another, we harm ourselves. In cherishing other beings, we lift up all. In recognizing the land as sacred, we have a chance to save the planet.

When we experience ourselves as connected to all things, profound healing takes place. Debra Hillary has had such experiences. In Finding the Shaman, Debra Hillary reveals her path to becoming Rainbow Medicine Woman. She tells of her life-choices, how she came to create a blended family while she grew spiritually, much the same as an aging river "finds a different way…to flow naturally". If you are lucky enough to have met Hillary, you will hear her voice leap from the pages, encouraging us to "live our lives with love, integrity and passion."

Enjoy the journey!

- Carolyn Nesbitt, PhD, Registered Psychologist

Preface

Walking a spiritual journey awakens our true self, through life experience and various degrees of trauma.

There lies the Shaman, sometimes buried or just below the surface.

How do you know that you are a Shaman?

We are all born spiritual beings with a special light.

Our soul contains the memories and past experiences of our countless lives.

And so, it begins, this is the difficult part. Navigating our life path, choosing all the lessons that we must learn from one life on to the next.

Unfortunately, there is no map to guide us. We must chart our own course on instinct and intuition.

Cellular memory coded in our DNA is one clue.

Uncovering our true self or listening to the signs that our body keeps telling us over and over again, like that nagging pain in the neck...or some kind of physical pain, sickness or disease.

Finding all parts of our selves to make a whole balanced being.

This is part of what a Shaman does, helps people to retrieve lost aspects of ones self.

A Shaman can go to other levels and travel between spirit world and this world.

And, has great capacity and understanding of the relationship between the worlds and human existence.

Experience, Knowledge and Wisdom, these are the fundamentals of our existence.

Here is where you can access the information you need in order to begin.

In your DNA the coding is there. In the memory of our own cells are the clues we require to track our path of truth and enlightenment. Our body is very sensitive in assisting us on this quest, the body will also give you clues as you go along on your journey, which way to go or not to go. The body is a complex system with built in sensory intelligence that is connected to our beginnings as humans.

The Nervous system must be calm and regulated for us to find our way efficiently, otherwise we end up going in circles.

Our mind, is it friend or foe?

The mind is an asset with its sharpness and library files full of information. Knowing this, we keep it in check, so that the ego will allow us to be balanced and humble. The Mind is powerful and mighty, but remember it does not control us. It is a part of the whole.

Our Spirit, our will, the light of our being, located in our hearts, this is the essence of our souls, keeping us on this journey of discovery, similar to a compass, it knows when and how to prompt us.

Free to choose the way in which we live our lives, with love, integrity and passion.

This is an art and a practice, to live with an open heart, to trust yourself and others. Following your own inner guidance system to freedom.

This is a peek in to my personal journey of self-discovery and healing journey. Remembering who I am... a Shaman of the Ages.

Blessings! Rainbow x

"All My Relations"

CHAPTER 1

IN THE BEGINNING-
TRAINING GROUND

I chose a whole family unit, with great wisdom and knowledge of human conditions.

Strong willed parents, who would teach me to be strong and fight for me too.

My family was comfortably well off, yet hard working.

I was born in the early sixties, a great time of change was occurring on the planet.

A revolution was about to begin…. a change in consciousness.

Many of the baby boomers came in awake, with open hearts and wanting to heal the damage from the past two world wars.

The language of this generation - was the music of pure genius by design, this would change the world.

It would instill a template for all the generations to follow.

Music has this affect on the young, to inspire, to question, to be themselves. To fight for what to believe in and what is the truth.

As leaders came in to power, these wise men and women stood up for change, they were also taken out of play just as quick.

The sixties was a volatile time, full of sorrow. The more we opened up and saw, the more we escaped into a world of love and color.

At this time there was a great mind and heart expansion happening too.

Drugs of all kinds were readily available to dive into another place and time. Escaping the pain and suffering that was all around us.

This was going on in the outside world and in my little world,

I witnessed pain and suffering from my parents generation, as they trying to forget the past...through picket fences in the suburbs and cocktail parties every weekend.

Creating a microclimate of false protection and far from harmony.

It was some sort of coping with what they had experienced growing up post war.

They were the Fallout Generation and carried this in their DNA.

As, the 1970's rolled around more change, we moved to the inner city, big homes filled with kids, we were a small family of 4 kids, average was 8-10 kids per house.

On our street we had plenty of kids to play with.

Then the big world came to our street…the FLQ October crisis 1970, we lived on a street in downtown Ottawa, with Members of Parliament and Senators next door, so the Army and Tanks and big guns arrived.

We thought it was cool, not really understanding, what it was all about. It was a very traumatic event in Canadian History. Our innocence of a wholesome land was shattered by horror and murder.

The following spring, another trauma occurred, my parents separated. After all the fighting, it was a bit of a relief.

I was learning and observing and coping with all of this unsettling information.

Luckily, my Grandparents were around, my mother's Mother was a healer and psychic. She recognized something in me and gave me her stone medicine collection to get me interested in the connection to the healing properties of the stones.

She would influence my life many years later, as I modeled how she lived and taught people how to enrich their lives through movement and art, health and wellbeing.

My father's parents, were also big influences, my Grandfather had show horses. I quickly connected with these beautiful animals in a spiritual sense.

Learned to listen to them, communicate with them, by watching him interact and talk with them. I had many teachers and mentors, of course not really knowing at the time, but was able to piece it all together later, understanding the knowledge that they were passing on to me was sacred and would awaken in me when the time was right.

We were fortunate that my Grandfather had purchased an island on a beautiful lake in Quebec, just outside of Ottawa, Hull region. The Algonquin Nation previously occupied this land.

It was a special place and would be the touchstone or constant in my young life to my adult life.

This is the place that I would awaken this gift of being connected to all of nature, Mother Earth and all her creatures.

Knowing at a young age that I felt the pulse or heartbeat of the Earth and all the creatures that live here.

Truthfully, I felt different and mostly misunderstood.

I would soon discover that the landscapes, and the spirits of sacred places that I would visit would begin to communicate with me and yes, awaken this inner knowing.

With all of the chaos in the family, there were moments of clarity. My parents brought us skiing every weekend to Camp Fortune in the Gatineau Hills.

Where, I became very focused on my physical expression of downhill skiing, it was a passion, and I channeled all my energy into it, going fast, than faster.

Where, I would excel and feel this sense of freedom like no other.

I also, stayed involved in horses for several years, as my father bought a farm, where I would further my connection to the land and animals and all that was involved in working a farm.

It was a great experience to be on the farm learning the fragility and beauty of life in balance. And, to feel the connection of the land and everything that lived from it.

I had experienced many aspects of life in these formative years, now I could put much of what I had learned to practice as I was coming of age.

I did experience and witness a lot of trauma in my family. I don't remember all the details, but my body has recorded much of what happened.

For an example, one day my father loaded us all up on the tractor for an adventure.

It was early spring and the fields were muddy and wet, my youngest sister was in the front loader and the rest of my siblings and I were scattered in different spots on the tractor.

All of a sudden there was a loud bang at the front of the tractor. My sister had fallen out of the loader and she was run over by the tractor. I thought she was dead, I flew 10 ft. in the air from the back of the tractor and picked her up from the mud and began running for the house. This was the Nervous system reaction of survival, run, run. You are not safe.

She was ok, she sunk into the muddy soil, she was 5 and I was 14. This was one of many scary events that happened to us.

There was definitely, Post-Traumatic stress affecting my Nervous System from early on, as it was passed down in the DNA of my Parents, Grandparents and generations before them as well.

Dangerous and daring deeds… the need for speed and chancing the odds.

It was hard wired into my being. I was not afraid to go fast. Putting everything on the line for a feeling of losing control and than somehow pulling it back to barely in control.

Wow! What a fantastic feeling, lots of adrenaline pumping through my veins to get me from the top to bottom. Beating the fastest time to beat.

This type of activity requires some sort of blind faith.

Knowing that you are protected and excepting of the possible consequences too.

All of the sports I loved involved speed and skill.

Skiing fast became my drug.

I had a gift in this sport. I kept fine tuning it.

I competed in ski racing. I let go of all the others sports and began to fixate on the speed.

It was all I wanted to do. I would skip school and go skiing.

It was practical and compact I could go anywhere with this sport.

I started to work in the local ski shops to get equipment. I saw this as my ticket to anywhere… but I had to finish High School first. So, how could I expedite this?

I would find a way to fulfill my passion for skiing and escape the chaos and pain.

CHAPTER 2 *

FULL CONNECTION TO DISCONNECTION

As, I was approaching eighteen, almost finished high school, I had my first out of body experience.

It seemed like a dream, but I was awake and flying around my room able to view my body as a shell. I did go somewhere, but returned back to my room, I was fearful that I might not come back to this body. This was extraordinary and unique, so I thought. Many of us have had this out of body experience, but discount it as a dream or a one of …that never happens again. This is connection to something from the past. Something, very familiar, before we are born, our spirit soars so high through the sky. Waiting to be born again to experience this life as a human.

I was ready to begin this awakening as part of my journey…

The very next week I was off to England to study at a University North of London as a credit course for my final year of high school. I was away for 4 months.

This was a solo journey that would change me forever.

When I arrived, it was very familiar. I recognized places and some people too.

My creative self stepped forward to open the door to another piece of me that I was unaware that was even there. The poetry poured out of me.

As, I travelled up country to an old part of England to visit some of Brittan's literary greats, final resting places. I encountered many spirits, ghosts and apparitions too.

They were everywhere I looked.

So, I began to drink more Guinness beer. Not really letting on what I had witnessed, no one would believe me.

Then I remembered, that I had experienced something like this when I was young, going to Camp in Algonquin Park, Ontario.

It was Native Spirits in the trees, bad ones, Fireballs.

No one else saw them but me.

I was connected to the Spirit world...

I had not forgotten how to see, the spirits are there all the time. I was sensitive to this energy. Picking up on this would help me navigate my journey many times in my life.

As, I learned of my gifts, I kept them hidden and secretly locked away deep inside of my heart and soul.

Sometimes, revealing them through creative aspects, painting or dance. And channeled this energy into ski racing, my outlet, my soul speaking to the world.

I noticed, that as I grew older, so did the frustrating; the anger was building and not being channeled for the best possible outcome. I was short with everyone.

I had lots of groups of friends, but I moved around not really belonging anywhere, feeling freedom to roam in and out of this social reform, this suited my butterfly personality.

At Eighteen, I meet my first husband at a friend's end of year ski party and saw into the future, the knowing was so clear.

I told him that we would have children together. This knowing scared him into disappearing, for several years.

I disappeared too, out West to the Mountains, to fulfill my passion for skiing and connecting to the mountain energy.

I went to Banff, Alberta to fulfill this desire to be skiing everyday in the mountains, to feel that closeness to The Creator.

Where I felt safe and protected, I belonged somewhere.

Escaping the low vibration and be above it all.

And, I would come to Whistler on tour of the West with my ski Team.

Upon, arriving it felt like home, not wanting to leave this breathe taking place.

Knowing, that someday I would return here, gave me a sense of calm.

So, after 3 years of being away from home, skiing out west, I would return to support my mother.

She experienced a tragic trauma and loss of her boyfriend through a drowning.

I held her up, some how trying to heal the pain that she felt.

We went to university together to heal, replace the pain and gather knowledge.

I studies Mass Communications and Film at Carleton University in Ottawa. Than discovered the radio station at the university and connected my voice and creative expression with this outlet.

I had my own Motown show on CKCU 93.1 I really enjoyed this and found the other studies overwhelming.

But stayed to complete almost 2 years of study.

Than, a chance meeting, after my return from the mountains, four years later... I reconnected with the boy I had met at that ski party.

We became great friends and travelling partners seeing many exotic places over the years before children. We travelled to Greece, Italy, Australia, and many more places around the globe.

I worked in Real Estate for a few years and than worked in the High end Jewelry business for years, before we decided to have children.

This human experience would soon reveal that there is work to do and through relationship I would learn hard and fast on heartbreak, overwhelm and what co-dependency looked like.

We had both experienced trauma and dealt with it differently.

Mine would be outwardly and his was inwardly.

We married in 1988, I gave birth to our first son, (1990) and this was a very happy time.

I was in my glory with a beautiful happy healthy child, going through the motions of my patterning from my child hood.

I had a template similar to my parents.

Fairly, good coping skills socially and with family.

But, suffered in silence as I began to notice that my husband was not doing as well with the pressure of life, family and responsibilities.

The wheels of the cart began to get wobbly and break down. The cart was about to explode.

The frustration started to mount and create a distancing within the partnership.

As, I was trying to hold it all together with band- aids. It really takes two to make it work or not work.

Sometimes, we cling to something that no longer serves us for our best and highest goodness.

This was one of those times. Out of fear, I was clinging to this relationship, knowing deep down this would become destructive for both of us.

And then, my second son was born (1992). I had two beautiful healthy boys.

11

It kept the obvious from happening for another year.

This was a very hard and difficult emotional time in my life. I felt very alone and sad.

I blamed myself and saw this as a huge failure.

But, once the shock of it wears off, you start to see the truth.

Making the decision to leave lifted a great weight of my shoulders.

I was not responsible for someone else's healing.

And I could let go of trying to fix someone else.

For the first time, I recognized my own strength and walked away with confidence in my actions.

Knowing that this was the right thing to do.

As, I let go I knew that I had to do this for my boys as much as I needed to do it for myself.

To stop the patterning and programming from continuing on through to the next generation.

CHAPTER 3 *

FRESH START IN THE GATINEAU HILLS

The boys and I would start a new life in the Gatineau Hills. Close to the ski hills and nature. I had friends and a support system in place.

I taught the boys how to ski and they loved it. They were 1 and 3 years old at the time.

We would ski almost every weekend and every night, they had night skiing at Camp Fortune.

I transitioned into being a single parent with small children. I would then start my spiritual awakening, away from trying to fix someone else.

The focus would shift me, into supporting my children the best way I could.

There would be lots of learning and growing in this period, (1994-1998) four years of letting go and becoming self sufficient.

Self-reliant, stronger and more empowered with the direction that my life would take, to assist in also guiding my two sons in the right direction for them to connect to their intended life paths.

This is where the soul starts to activate the memories and gifts, knowing what path to take.

Usually, when you are up against the wall, so to speak.

Life intensifies the need to use your instincts of survival.

Listening to the guidance of our own being and wisdom within. What is truly for our best and highest good will appear and reinforce the true path of existence.

During, this expansive spiritual growth period, I would start to connect with my power and creative gifts and see more through my intuition (Third Eye Chakra).

I would have more awakenings and visions, as this time frame was a portal of Universal energy and knowledge that was coming through to a few light beings that could handle this frequency.

I began to see my path more clearly.

I had experience with the jeweler business and decided to delve more into to the Holistic side of the jewellery business.

I started a small company to support my family with the Native Inspired Gemstone Jeweler creations with healing properties.

Moonstone Jewellery would uncover the stories and legends of many aboriginal cultures.

Including my own heritage. As, I would make and create the jewellery at night as my boys slept.

Most of these neckpieces were made from natural gemstones that had unique healing properties to heal people on a very slow vibration.

My Grandmother had passed the stone medicine on to me to share.

So, I knew what most of the gems were used for intuitively, and would channel the sequence and combine the stones, which had a specific vibration or frequency for healing the bearer of theses items.

Each piece had a name and story with it, to increase its potentency and vibration.

This jewellery line was well received by Museums and Galleries across Canada and people from all over the world purchased these one of a kind pieces. Some people would recognize the name or frequency in each piece as the key to their healing journey.

This is how I supported my boys and I for four years.

Lots of sleepless nights and having to travel to get the purchase orders took a toll on my energy level and my physical wellbeing.

I suspected that on a sub-conscious level, I was preparing for a huge shift.

My being felt the rumblings of something big was going to take place soon.

And there would be no going back to the way things use to be...

CHAPTER 4 *

RELOCATION TO THE WEST (RETURNING HOME)

I travelled across Canada and down to the southwestern U.S to promote my new line of jewellery, every fall and spring to bring back orders to fill. My boys and family would help me put the orders together and sometimes help me name the pieces. Each item had a sacred name and meaning and healing properties attached.

This was the Stone Medicine coming through in the frequency of each piece. The centerpiece of each necklace was the activation part and the rest of the necklace would assist with the total healing that the bearer would need.

This jewellery was very well received in the West. So, I would spend more time travelling to Calgary, Banff, Vancouver and Whistler. I still had great contacts and friends in all of these places.

I would return home to Chelsea and Ottawa, feeling a real sense of missing the West. Every time, would be harder to leave the vibration and beauty of the West.

I began to question the feeling in my body and mind. It was getting more difficult to live where we were. My body let me know. I was forced to listen. Stop! Now! Cannot move, too much Pain! The pain body had kicked in.

I was not listening very well, trying to stubbornly push through the obvious.

So, The Creator and I became closer and I worked through the pain and suffering, by letting the love and healing to occur.

I chose the route of alternative healing.

Creator said, "This is a lesson you need to know and explore, so one day you can help

Others to know, that they too can take control of there own healing journey."

Wow, what a journey it was, from not being able to move out of crippling pain for 4 weeks to extreme nerve pain in lower back to going back to skiing in 1.5 months. I was suffering from a ruptured disc, old injury and old memory pain.

I was, first seen by an Orthopedic Surgeon. He said, "We need to operate and remove that disc". I told him, "No way will I go under the knife". I told him, " that I would be back 100% healed and able to walk and run and have a good quality of life". The odds that he had given me, with or with out surgery was 50/50 you would be able to walk.

So, I started with bodywork, connected the emotional pain with the body pain and released some of it.

It was a great start, good connection to Creator, motivated me to connect with my Healing Journey of self- discovery of the old knowledge that was there, the whole time.

To come through, that experience was very liberating and empowering.

I began, to be a seeker of the truth and search for deeper connection with people and myself and read books, to be inspired by others who have had similar experiences with the divine.

It charted a whole new path for me. And I had my boys, to give me that inner strength to keep going strong and live with passion.

So, the more I listened to my inner self, the more opportunities would be presented to me.

In the fall of 1997, I was invited by The Royal Canadian Mint to be at this Native Artist Gathering in Scottsdale, Arizona. "Spirits in the Sun", was the name of the conference.

Where, I would meet many of the very best and talented Aboriginal artists in Canada.

I met someone at the conference, who would invite me to the Haida Gwaii Islands of the most Northern Coast of British Columbia.

Also, known as the "Isles of Wonder", that would change my life path forever...

September 1998, I tied this in with my business trip to the west, but spent weeks away this time to explore and listen to the land. This is truly one of the most awe-inspiring places on the planet. This land heals with its timelessness and beauty. The land, its people and animals spoke to me in the most profound way. Really spoke to my spirit or higher self.

With such wisdom and knowledge, I was compelled to listen and be silent and journey by myself on a vision quest, where the Raven would comfort me and protect me and guide me back to self.

This was the beginning of "My Rainbow Journey".

The elders told me that I was to be here on the coast and coastal mountains to learn of my culture and heritage of being a Medicine healer. There will be many teachers and mentors to guide you home. You are needed here to hold the vibration and frequency for the planet.

I am thinking to myself, am I dreaming this… is this really happening now? It took me a while to have it sink in, but this was happening and it would happen very quickly, so I did not have time to analyze the process. Acting, purely on inner guidance from Spirit.

It was true… I got back to Vancouver and headed right to Whistler.

I got a job and a place to rent and phoned my mother, who was looking after the boys.

I said, "We are moving here to be in the mountains. I am on my way back home to pack us up and move to Whistler to start a new life". So, we moved to Whistler as my boys had the passion for skiing too!

The boy's Father and I agreed on the divorce settlement of letting me take them to Whistler, BC. He said, "I trust you to do the right thing, for you and the boys."

We would all thrive in this new environment. And so, it would be one of the best decisions that I had ever made. The boys would take to this new place like they had always been here, apart of the mountain culture, drinking up everything that was in front of them.

We were living in a tiny 1 Bedroom suite, but what a view! Mountains Spectacularly covered in white snow. The house overlooked the lake and we could see both Mountains everyday, calling to us.

Everything fell into place, we were happy and loving our new environment. Family would come and visit often. The boys, Father would come out and spend time with them too.

I worked on the mountain teaching skiing everyday and some nights, where I would teach Native arts to visitors children and on the weekends the boys would come with me to work and ski with great coaches, explore the mountain.

Honing their ski skills every time they would be on the mountain. I would sometimes, take them out of school to ski with me on big powder days.

It was truly amazing to watch as we headed down the mountain in the deep powder, we were compared to a pod of dolphins, going up and down under the snow. It was like time stopped, as they followed.

Then, they started to pass me and I marveled at their abilities as they continued to get more in tune with the mountain and the snow and seemed to have this sixth sense with this environment.

As they developed their skills on the mountain, I was developing my intuition and creativity through painting and writing.

My physical self was tuning into subtle energies and vibrations. I was close to the Creator on top of the mountains, in a higher frequency.

Higher self was connected to creator. So, I could absorb the information easier. I was really connecting to my spirit self and physical self to heal and accept who I really was.

Oh, and I also really enjoyed skiing powder on the mountain everyday.

CHAPTER 5 *

TEACHERS APPEAR

As, I began to realize my connection to the Creator and Spirit world… the path became more defined.

I attracted many spiritual beings to my life and the teachers appeared, one by one for different aspects of myself to learn.

Not only how to be… but, how to heal those parts of myself that had been fractured or hurt or taken from me.

Let the true healing begin.

Living in a place like Whistler, you are surrounded by beauty and you start to connect back to your original self, connected more to what is for your best, to give you more joy and peace of mind.

What, I was attracting was my soul family members. We had great gatherings and feasts, ceremonies and celebrations. This is a special community of people.

Honoring one another in a very sacred way.

This is what, my sons will remember, how to treat others with great respect and love. I was creating a template for them to base future friendships and gatherings from. How to really connect with people.

I did not know it at the time, but that is exactly what it was.

Creating a new code to live by... these were very happy times for us, just the three of us.

I had saved up enough money to finally purchase a home for us in (2000). I worked two jobs for one whole year. My Mother helped too! And we had our little house on the hill in Pemberton, BC.

A farming community just twenty minutes from Whistler and a very spiritual land where thousands of First Nations people lived before anyone else inhabited it.

The Elders told me, that a century ago this land was prosperous and thriving.

The first people were living off the land and rivers and succeeded to co-exist with their environment.

They lived in harmony with everything and used the medicine from the land that would keep them connected and continue to honor the sacredness of the Mother Earth.

The Lilwat and N'QuatQua Nations are inner coastal Salish living in the traditional Territory of the Squamish-Lillooet region.

I began to remember who I was, feeling that I was on the right track. The memory was recorded in my cellular makeup of my DNA.

I made it work, having a suite downstairs, having people live with us to pay the mortgage. That financial stress was not so great.

I still had something for the boys to call home and we didn't have to move every six months. We could have our many gatherings and people over.

I could have my art workshops in my living room. The house became a gathering place for the clan on many occasions. The best and most memorable gathering was for my fortieth birthday party. October 2001.

Families arrived all day to celebrate and than by 7:30pm everyone had arrived with musical instruments and pots and spoons for a proper jam session.

We made the most amazing music together, an orchestra from the heavens. This would go on, until the wee hours of the morning. I will never forget the elevated and strongly supported feeling, that I had that day.

It was pure magic. Thanks, to all those talented music makers that evening for filling my heart with love.

My teachers were in all forms, big and small. I would learn in relationships with boyfriends. I would be put to the test by my children, at work and by countless others that would give me gifts of knowledge and teach me how to be myself.

How to: respond to the world around me with respect and humility.

Over the ten years, before I would meet my second husband. I learned my hard lessons on all levels, mentally, physically and emotionally. Letting go of all the patterning that I had absorbed as a child, some good, some not so helpful.

Letting go of the trauma, going deeper to find myself was what I had to do.

Than, I was brought to The Elders of The Lilwat nation to learn my Medicine.

Sweat lodge ceremony, Sundance, fasting, smudging, connection to the Earth and all its creatures become part of you as you engage in this practice and ceremonial existence.

The Good Red Road.

The more I learned about the traditions and scared ceremonies I knew that this was also part of me.

I knew this to be the truth.

These are The Scared Teachings that have been passed down from generation to generation in all aboriginal cultures.

Being totally connected to all that lives and breathes on Mother Earth, under the protection of Father Sky, the Creator.

I would experience an enormous physical hit. Very bad mountain bike crash, August (2001) that would leave me in the fog for months and lingered for years.

From all of the previous ski crashes from the past, this would create post trauma to the brain.

This was harder to recover from. The Brain does not like the repeated hits to the head.

This was a physical setback, as well as suffering financial ruin; I had no recollection of time and space and missed payments to the banks for everything life had to throw at me.

No compassion from the institutions. This was a hard lesson.

Creator had brought me to my knees again, begging for forgiveness and pleading for some help and clarity.

How do I fudge my way out of this nasty mess?

"There is no easy way out." "Start fresh, start from here. Forget, all that you have learned". The Creator said.

"Start from the beginning as a human. Start with yourself, gather new knowledge, start recalling the old knowledge, go back to your beginnings as a healer of the people and the land."

"You can remember through your creative process, Paint your past. Your future will be revealed". The Creator said.

So, I started to paint after I would come out of Sweat lodge ceremony, I would remember my visions and paint them, the paintings would reveal lots of old teachings and reveal to me my true self as a Shaman of the ages.

The Elders would encourage me to go deeper to find my truth. My path and soul purpose was great, they told me and had been telling me, since my trip to the Haida Nation years earlier.

I had much to learn and experience.

I felt like a newborn in a glass house, so fragile and vulnerable. Afraid to break, let go, express the deep emotion inside, the pent up frustration of living this way.

I withdrew into myself and re-evaluated my life and where I was headed.

After the head injury, I became more sensitive to energy and could see more of the unseen. The clouds were lifting.

The lightness had returned. And, I was more hopeful of my life path and everything in it.

So, the process began to make this my new reality.

I was now inspired to make my first film. It was a documentary called, "Trading Secrets".

I gathered the talent and the elders and we started filming the stories, the beliefs and traditions of how to practice this sacredness.

We started filming in Vancouver, BC at an Event that was "Drumming in Peace" attracting people from all over the world, sharing their Drum medicine from all cultures.

There were 5000 people in attendance. It was at the Plaza of Nations, September 22/2001.

One week after the attack in New York 9/11. It was a very powerful an emotional event. We connected with some amazing people, who are in the film sharing their wisdom.

There were many signs that this was meant to be.

The film was celebrated by many and received well, debuting at The Wetama Celebration Native festival in Whistler in 2002.

Showcasing Native culture around Whistler.

But, I was side tracked to getting it to go further. Life and letting others affect my inner guidance and my path, "Distracting Drama" I call it.

I am a bridge builder, but I could not make the connection yet, there was too much hurt and resentment still.

It is all about the timing and when to deliver the message.

The world was not ready for this information.

It is a beautiful and special film dedicated to all aboriginal people of the world.

It will be shared...When the time is right.

CHAPTER 6 *

Meeting My Life mate

This chapter could also be a whole other book on its own, but this is the history. The Creator gives us these Life lessons to better our existence or to take from these experiences great learning, and in relationship, is where we will learn the most important lessons.

And most likely, where our best teachers are.

So, as Creator would have it, I would draw in and attract one of the best teachers of my life so far… my second husband.

Whom, I met on top of an eight thousand foot Peak in the Coastal Mountain Range (April 2003).

We were with two different backcountry ski groups headed for the same Peak to ski fresh powder that had fallen overnight.

We all stayed in the same backcountry cabin, and we're delighted to see the sun come out and reveal the snow caped Peaks with fresh snow.

What a day it would be. Bluebird blue sky!

As our groups reached the Peak at the same time, we glanced at one another and said, "Where do I know you from?" We recognized one another from somewhere some other time. Trying hard to recall the meeting.

We had distanced ourselves to chat from the two groups and noticed that it felt like we were there all by ourselves, so it seemed.

There was this intense exchange of energy, I had not experienced before.

Almost like a merging.

And we noticed that the group of people also noticed this intensity of energy and commented on it among themselves.

So, we broke our dome of silence and returned to our respective groups. And had the ski run of our lives.

We exchanged phone numbers that day, both saying,

"Stay in touch."

I could not stop thinking of him from that day and would look for him everywhere, to possibly have another chance to connect further.

No sign of him, no phone calls.

I hoped that he would call, as I was instructed to let him come to me, by the Creator.

I had to be patient with this one. There was a very good reason he had to come to me.

For many months friends had told me that they saw a child around me, waiting to come through.

I had hoped that I would or could conceive another child, my boys were older now 12-15 at the time.

They were getting really good at skiing and competed in all the local events of free skiing, slope style and half pipe.

The sponsors were starting to take notice of these 2 little rippers.

Life was starting to change in a real positive direction.

And, still no sign of this mystery man from the mountaintop.

I carried on with my life and Shamanic studies and furthered my healing journey with many ceremonies.

I was training to be a Sun Dancer that spring.

I started out as a supporter and than experienced the training of what was involved to be a Sun Dancer.

This would be one of the hardest tests I would do in my life on all levels.

There is a lot of preparation to be committed to this Practice.

First, get all of the tools that you will need to be a Sun Dancer, physically, mentally, emotionally and spiritually.

So I did, many Sweat lodge ceremonies. Made smudge, gathered medicines had a sacred Drum, rattle and feathers.

Prepare your body, eat good food, and get lots of sleep and no drugs or alcohol.

Understand, that you will sacrifice yourself for the good of the people.

To pray for them, to sweat for them, to fast for them, to suffer on all levels, taking there prays and pain to the spirit world.

I was under the guidance and protection of the Blackfoot Nation. They came to the Lilwat-Squamish territory to help us decide if this was our intended path.

I had committed to try this path, and was willing to learn and have Creator decide if this was my path to be a Sun Dancer for the people.

We started on the Thursday night, big feast and lots of supporters encouraging the dancers, giving us bundles and gifts for this next four days, they would be difficult.

The first Sweat Lodge ceremony was six hours and very hot, no food or water for four days.

Waking up the first morning, I did lick the dew off my tent.

I was so thirsty, we keep busy making a fire to dry our clothes and gathered cedar to make smudge.

There were mostly women and 2 men training for Sun Dance ceremony.

Some of them had done a Sundance before.

I listened to the questions and asked a few too. People were mostly, introspective as to get through their own stuff was challenging.

In the Sweat lodge, people had to surrender, and let go of their pain and conditioning. Many were sick or crying.

I mostly, sang and wanted to be strong for them. I was not willing to let go just yet. I had much to learn, what it was to be a Sun Dancer.

This was just a small part I had the privilege and honor to experience what the Sun Dancer must endure.

I did suffer physically from the lack of hydration and my hormones were messed up for sometime, but I learned so much about myself and have such great respect for people who are called to service as brave and courageous Sun Dancers.

Many Blessings and thanks to The Dancers and their supportive families and communities. They keep are hopes and dreams alive with this tradition.

So, in retrospect this was a great part of my journey back to self. As, I was shown how to be respectful, grateful and The humble student. I have had some amazing teachers along the way, as they shared with me their wisdom of the Scared Teachings.

So, as I was busy taking care of my spiritual self, the universe was plotting to arrange my mountaintop man drive by my house to see if I still lived there.

I saw him drive by several times. He was obviously trying to get the courage to ask me out.

It took him about 8 months, from the time he meet me on the mountaintop.

He than, phoned a few weeks later, to see if I would meet him for a coffee at the bottom of the mountain after work?

I had no hesitation,

"Yes, that would be perfect!!!" Oh My God, now what?

My heart and mind raced, now what do I do?

Am I ready for this?

I knew that once I stepped into this, it would happen very fast. It was an instant connection.

And, there was no time to waste as my little angel spirit was around me trying to come through as I was running out of time to conceive a child at 43.

This spirit had been around me for several years patiently waiting for the right Daddy to show up.

We started dating at the beginning of the year, 2004 and I was pregnant with in 2 months.

He kept asking me to move in, it took until July. The boys and I moved into his house in Pemberton, than in August we were married and by end of November we welcomed our beautiful little daughter.

I went into the hospital to have a baby and instantly we were a family of seven, my two boys, his daughter and son, and our newest little addition as we all lived together in Pemberton.

It was a big adjustment for all of us.

Blending a family is one of the most challenging things to do in life. And, this is most difficult for all members to accept.

And, we all lived on the top floor of house 1200 sq. ft. as the suite was rented.

We soon realized, that we needed the whole house, as the kids were getting older and we all needed more breathing room. These next few years would put our relationship to the ultimate test.

Could we survive all the complexities of a blended family? Time would tell and show us how to heal.

With all of the older kids spending more time in Whistler at friends houses and the boys were travelling lots to compete at Freeski events around the world.

We had more time to get to know each other and work out relationship issues.

I was back at work on the mountain and started to work at The Oracle in Whistler doing Medicine Card readings and healings for people.

I started to work back on my spiritual self as my world became increasingly more stressful and demanding mental, physically and emotionally at home.

All of the kids pushed us to show up and be our best, challenged us and taught us many lessons to remember.

They were all great teachers.

And now our youngest daughter is challenging us.

I was not so thankful at the time, but now I can say it was all worth it.

I am a better person and now, I have a greater understanding of being a good parent.

And I have more understanding of being a parent.

Show compassion and love from every angle, and know that I can be better and more tolerant.

As, they are all finding their way to be amazing human beings.

The relationship that I now have with all of our children is better than I could have imagined.

There is constant change and learning in all relationships and it has made my relationship with my husband better because we have come through lots of difficult things together and will continue to grow, as we learn and get to the next phase of our relationship.

What I have learned from this is don't give up, keep trying to see your way through and you will find an opening that has many rewards.

Stay positive in relationship and seek the answer.

What is the lesson here?

Don't take on others issues. All of the hardship is emotional baggage from past relationship that is referred to the existing ones.

LET GO of the past traumas, so you can see your own self in a healthy relationship with yourself first, and than the rest is easier.

Able to communicate with others with out the drama.

Not to get triggers by others.

Notice how you react or don't react to others.

You will feel more regulated and balanced yourself by being more aware of your Nervous System.

This is what relationship has taught me...

As I practice this, I am now checking in with myself first before I come back with something that I will regret later.

Like, a backlash or reactionary response.

Take your time and orientate yourself, come back into your body and be here now to have clarity of body and mind.

Remember that you are not responsible for healing that person or taking on their issues.

Keep coming back to self. You deserve to be healed.

CHAPTER 7 *

BALANCING ACT

I am a mother, wife, sister, daughter, healer, Shaman, teacher and friend.

I take all of these rolls in stride… they are parts of me not all of me.

It is difficult to keep all of these going everyday and work a full time job as well as doing things for yourself.

Society has put many expectations on us, to be good at all of these rolls, all at the same time.

And, as the pace of life gets quicker, we feel the pressure to keep up more.

I am constantly searching for balance everyday.

Where is that center to keep me on an even keel?

In my experience, hitting the wall and burning out has happened, no energy to give to myself.

I have been looking after everyone else's needs and caring for family members, friends, clients, co-workers and perfect strangers.

And, it happened even after all the peeling back of the layers, there was more to peel and reveal, my body started to shut down and go into Freeze mode a few years ago, after a couple of traumatic events in a row.

The physical shut down, affected my legs, they felt like heavy bricks. Overall aches and pains through out my whole body.

Fog brain and not able to stay focused and no energy.

One of the girls that I worked with recognized that I had Post Traumatic Stress Disorder (PSTP) because she had suffered from it for many years as well.

So, that day I phoned my other friend who was working through her trauma and was going for an appointment that day to see the trauma specialist using Somatic Experience practice, so she got me an appointment right after her.

This is what I had been waiting for, a break through in my healing journey.

Something that connected all the dots, it was bridging Science with Spirituality.

To better explain with a specific language, what I do and how this can help others.

For me this was the Rainbow Medicine that would heal me and show me how to assist others on their healing journeys.

The demand is great for people seeking guidance on how to heal them selves.

I was able to get some helpful tools that would help me regulate my fragile Nervous System.

So, I began to study this Practice, Somatic Experience discovered by DR. Peter Levine, as to get more tools and keep letting go of my own trauma.

Some of it is from this life, some from many life times ago and some in the DNA.

Our body, mind and spirit are directly affected by this negative energy and sometimes displaced or trapped energy can cause problems and deep pain on all levels.

Like a volcano, the pressure can build, than there is an eruption of magma or emotions in humans can erupt.

Which is an uncontrollable amount all at once with no control as to how much is going to come out at any one time.

What happens to many people is that they get stuck in a highly charged state or stuck on shut off mode and they are not able to maintain a normal regulated nervous system.

This is how they cope with overload and desperation.

Because, the ability to feel something, anything is cut off.

So, they bring in what is readily available such as drugs and alcohol or obsessive-compulsive behaviors to cope.

The more I observe and study, the more I start to have a better understanding of how to look after myself and keep checking in on how my nervous system is coping.

If, I sense overwhelm, I have a couple of exercises that I do to come back to center and calm within.

So, what is the secret to keeping it all together and keeping your head and body from blowing up?

There is a way to find balance.

It is possible, but there is something that you must let go of in order to achieve this Mastery in your life.

This is a deep-rooted imprinting that has been passed on from generation to generation.

We have learned this behavior, and now we need to let it go and create a new way of doing things, that is more efficient and effective for our lives, to pass on this new way of being to our children so they can live more regulated happy lives.

Look at your Mother or Grandmother what are the things that they do that are similar?

And then look at your Father or Grandfather, what do you notice?

Than, see if you have any of those traits.

Notice that there are ones that you don't like and ones that you admire.

Being all of these things and to be good at any of them is not realistic and would total drive anyone to crazy town.

Where to begin:

Start with not judging yourself and give yourself a lot of credit for doing a good job.

Now, let go of the feeling of obligation to be perfect.

Let go of looking after everyone and there needs, put your needs first.

What do you need to make you happy? How does that feel?

This process is not an overnight success.

This is a practice to get everyone use to this new you and new way of doing things.

Don't do this cold turkey, start to take back yourself slowly so, there is time to integrate, into the new you.

This Letting Go will be a huge release of energy on your Nervous System so, go at your own pace and listen to your body. It will let you know how much you can push.

Be gentle with yourself!

You are taking back your power that was given away at your birth.

As you tune into this gift you are more and more empowered to share this with others.

But, Keep it for a while to revel in your spiritual freedom.

This is a compass of sorts to keep you on course of your intended spiritual path and purpose.

You will start to feel better and less stressed and way less chaotic.

The mind, body and spirit align in perfect harmony. This is a balanced existence, to enjoy life and all its glory.

If I had known this information earlier, I could have saved myself years of torment and struggle, but as a Shaman I experienced and explored the depths of internal turmoil and hardship so, I could understand the process of how to overcome and over through the Monkey on my back.

It is a Step-by-Step process, celebrate accomplishments, better life choices more clarity of who you are.

For many of us, Life has been full of ups and downs, trials and tribulations.

Why does it have to be so complicated?

Just, when you think you have it all figured out, here comes that curve ball right out of left field.

And your life has to shift. This is good meaning that there is movement.

Not staying stuck.

If you recognize the patterns you can slowly start to change what is not working and incorporate what is.

This is the key to being open to learning how to make a better life. As you shift the negative and release the trapped old trauma and programs, you can integrate the new ones into your being.

Then, you begin to function more calmly and make better choices and respond in tune with what is best for you.

Bring on a Happy Existence. "Be Happy"!!!

Open up yourself and your heart will be open to more acceptance and Love in all forms.

CHAPTER 8 *

WIDE AWAKE

Like the song, " I am wide awake, I am born out of The Lion's Den, don't need to pretend".

I am Wide Awake Now, free to be my true self.

I am gaining a deeper understanding of how to be and acknowledge my true self as who I am right now, and except the changes to come.

This state of being is helpful for my mind, body and spirit.

So, this is the real life test, can I step into the spotlight?

As humans this is hard wired into us.

We doubt our ability to be magnificent and beautiful.

Am I good enough?

Am I worthy to be a bright light, a shinning light for the whole world to see?

I have been training and preparing for this moment my whole life. This is the right time to show my true self to be the best I can be.

I am accomplishing this right now! I have been inspired to write my personal journey to share with others.

I can inspire, I can teach, I can keep learning to be open hearted and speak my truth.

Others have come before me to seek change and growth of our evolutionary development, not afraid to be their true selves.

Buddha was an ordinary person seeking the truth and found enlightenment.

And inspired change and continues to change peoples lives 25 centuries later.

A quote from one of my famous relatives, Sir Edmund Hillary said, when people would ask him. What made him climb the highest mountain in the world? He responded with this.

"People do not decide to be extraordinary, they decide to accomplish extraordinary things."

Something or someone can spark you to keep searching for you own truth. It is all around us.

I have found that the healing can be in the land. It heals us with is beauty and reflects it back to us.

Finding the clarity in knowing how to go about igniting your spiritual journey… is not easy.

It is having the courage to start somewhere, and believe in your dreams and desires to be a happy, healthy balanced being.

One of the things, I get my clients to do before we have a healing session.

I ask them to be really honest about what they what to let go of and what they want to attract into their lives?

Write on a piece of paper Let go of on the Left hand of page on the right hand write what you want in you life?

It is an exercise of bringing awareness to those things, bringing them to life. This is not goal setting.

In this knowing you can let go easier. Bring awareness to it.

As a ritual we safely burn them after to release this energy to the Creator.

As people let go, they become lighter and able to integrate new higher frequency energy into their being.

This process has to be gentle and slow as most of us have and carry trauma in the DNA, which affects the efficiency of our Nervous Systems.

The Healing also occurs with acknowledgement that PTSD or Post Traumatic Stress Disorder has affected many generations. This realization can benefit the healing process by forgiveness of past actions to yourself and others.

So, before we start we do an assessment of the Nervous system function.

Are they able to regulate or cope? Can the Sympathetic Nervous System come back down by activation of the Para-Sympathetic Nervous System?

If the system is fragile, we go to then providing a supportive environment and orientate them to this slowly to calm the Nervous System back to baseline.

And, I incorporate my Shamanic Tools, such as My Medicine drum, rattle, Smudge Ceremony burning of Sage or sweet-grass, crystal stone Medicine and feathers.

An environment with sacred objects to surround them in Traditional Medicine is the ultimate healing. This is the external environment and internally this happens for the client.

My Nervous System will communicate with their Nervous System and will automatically calm.

As I continue on this path, I have been able to combine my two passions of skiing and helping people all in one place, under Rainbow Medicine.

Working on the Mountain in Whistler allows me to connect with people from all over the world, to help them overcome their fears and obstacles that prevent them from learning and achieve a good quality of life.

I have had clients go into to full-blown panic right in front of me on the mountain.

I have recognized what they are experiencing and can calm them to regulate their Nervous Systems.

Then, we can continue to learn how to ski in a calm and regulated manner.

We can change and create new pathways in the brain to deepen the connection to our true selves.

"Be Who You Are...

Be Free to Chose How You Want to Live Your Life.

CHAPTER 9 *

WISDOM TEACHINGS

These are the Wisdom Teachings of White Buffalo Calf Women taught to me Rainbow Medicine Women.

We have much to learn and by understanding some of the traditional ways of living, we can all benefit.

Honoring the Mother Earth, Protecting Father Sky, respect for our Elders and Ancestors, teaching our children how to treat our environment, traditions and stories can be passed on.

We can see our lives come back into greater balance.

Learn to co-exist with all living creatures, take what you need, give back to the Earth.

Be Mindful of what you put in your body, choose good healthy lifestyle.

Be Kind to one another, be hopeful in achieving peace with in your heart.

Attract abundance and share your successes with others.

Than, there is the spiritual aspect of living in Harmony with all things.

This is referred to as The Good Red Road.

There are 7 ceremonies that have been gifted by White Buffalo Calf Women. Also known, as Lila Wakan to the Lakota.

I will tell you first of the Legend that has been passed down in the Lakota Nation for hundreds of years.

How the White Buffalo Calf Women came to be.

She is a Great Teacher of Wisdom and Knowledge.

She is a teacher of Patience and commitment to practicing the Sacred Rites.

First, bringing the Sacred Pipe Ceremony to the people.

It is said, that she appeared in front of two scouts that morning.

One was being lustful towards her, and she turned him to dust. The other one hide out of fear, she told him to go to the village and prepare for her visit to the people that next day.

She had a message of great importance. She told him, if he did this she would spare his life.

The scout returned to the village and told them of what he had seen.

He said, "She is the most beautiful women, he had ever seen. She is coming and wants everyone to gather to hear the teachings"...

The next day, she appeared to all of the people in the village.

All in white buckskin with beautiful dark black hair and white Buffalo fur around her. She was a vision of sacredness and beauty.

She than handed the Chief the Sacred Pipe with Sacred tobacco to be smoked and passed around offering prays to the Creator.

This was a great gift to the Lakota people to be connected to and honor the Creator and the ceremony to be shared with all of the people.

She than said, that she would return everyday with new teachings and ceremonies for the people.

As she walked away she turned into a White Buffalo Calf.

The White Buffalo Calf Women appeared and gifted many more Scared Rites, such as Keeping of the Soul, Purification known as the Sweat Lodge, Vision Quest, The Sundance, Puberty rite into Women hood and Blessing Ceremonies.

As she left, for the last time she said to the people that, she would one day return when the time was right…

That, there would be signs to signal her return to strengthen the people's belief and connection to the Creator and the land through the honoring ceremonies.

These ceremonies are being held all around the planet, but many have forgotten the sacred ceremonies.

Here is a channeled…

Message from White Buffalo Calf Women:

Blessed Ones, the deep healing is occurring on the planet now...

Awareness of what has been happening has been revealed

It is time to walk in your own beauty and elevate your

Vibration to new heights to reach the Rainbow frequency to

Inspire others to make the changes necessary to have a better

Existence for all living things on Planet Earth.

Peace... is within you and all around us.

Many Blessings!

CHAPTER 10 *

WITH MUCH GRATITUDE

One of the best ways, to be totally successful on your healing journey is to be filled with Gratitude for all beings, that have helped you in some way to find your Path and stay on it.

Honestly, I kept searching for what would work for me.

My path took a few different avenues until I found the right one... It was not a straight shot.

The road was full of twists and turns.

This journey was a Shaman's path of discovery.

I look to nature for some of the answers to explain life, take the river.

When a river is formed it flows straight, as it gets older, it starts to meander, it finds a different way to go around and change course.

The water always finds a way to flow naturally. And get to its deserved destination, reuniting with the waters of the oceans. And then do it all over again, repeating the cycle.

From Rain to river, back home to the big water, the ocean.

You are the only one who really knows what is best for you and your specific needs.

Your memories are stored in the cells of your DNA.

To access this important information, there is a key to unlocking your memories.

It is sometimes a combination of different healing modalities that will work and sometimes, one is all you need.

You will know which is best, as your body will let you know which is the right way. It will feel complete and make sense to your mind and body. Align with all that is you.

And, your higher self will confirm your Path and Purpose.

Listen to the subtleties you will know how to find your way.

I have had teams of people, that have supported me at any one time along my healing journey.

Thank you to the countless Bodyworkers, Massage and Physiotherapist Coaches and Teachers.

Humbly with gratitude, the Spiritual Teachers that reminded me that I had the knowledge to keep searching for the truth.

I would like to acknowledge the many animals that have helped me on my Spiritual quest as they have showing me, how to relate to the Earth and keep connected to being aware of my environment.

Thank you to all the elements Water, Air, Fire and Wind for providing life for me.

I honor the North, East, South and the West directions for all the good medicine.

I give thanks to the mountains and the oceans for giving me balance in my masculine and feminine self.

I would like to show my deepest appreciating and gratitude for Our Earth Mother "Gaia". For all that she commands.

As, she has shown me humility and how to share her messages to the people of the planet.

Here is one of the many messages she has shared with me:

I am Gaia herself, full of potential.
Affected by the cycles of the Moon,
Ebbing and flowing with the tides.

I am Gaia herself, marveling at
The Blueness of the Sky,
The flourishing of the forest.

I am Gaia herself, seeing the wonders of
The oceans, lakes and rivers,
Full of infinite Life.

I am Gaia herself protect me, from the polluters
And corporations who wish
To conquer, my precious existence.

I am Gaia, Honor, and Cherish and bless me.

Many thanks for all my Spirit Guides and Ancestors that have
been guiding me my whole life.

I am Thankful for the many natural plant and stone medicines
that have been given to me to share and show how they will help
people heal and facilitate their journeys.

I am full of gratitude and grace to have been totally connected
to The Creator, The many Masters and Angels that have been
so instrumental in keeping me going through their continues love
and support.

And, my own intuition and inner guidance system keeps leading
me to the right people every time.

And, even when it wasn't the right people I would still learn something from them.

I am so grateful for all of the people that have been in my life and the ones who are always there for me, unconditionally.

Many Thanks to the ones who have mentored, counseled, guided, healed, hurt, shunned, shammed, inspired, influenced, and directed me back to my true self.

It would not have been possible to find out who I was if not for all that I have experienced in this beautiful journey of my life so far...

I am truly blessed to have met and interacted with such amazing and inspiring beings from all over the world.

Thank you from the bottom of my heart for all the love and support of my family and good friends who have shown me encouragement and faith through out my entire existence.

There is no mystery to having a happy existence; you have your own truth inside of you.

You can create the journey you wish to live by living it and learning from each lesson, whether it is good or not so good.

Don't be afraid of making a mistake. Make as many as you can, so you can grow and learn. Be open to the Love that is around you and except yourself for who you are.

It is easy to reflect on where we have been.

But, our vision of where we are going seems so much more exciting, if we see it in a more positive light we can achieve great things for ourselves and others too.

Live your best Life… Start today, go out and do something that scares you a little bit.

Do something that you have always wanted to do? Learn how to ski or ride a bike.

Than do something creative like write a song or paint.

Now that you are on a roll... do something wonderful for yourself, cook and prepare a beautiful meal, as you would prepare for someone else.

Indulge yourself fully... you deserve it.

You can achieve greatness and your wildest dreams, as you wish it and dream it.

It can become a reality... You become who you truly are...

Amazing!!!

Many Blessings on your life Journey to uncovering your trueself!

About the Author

Debra Lee Hillary (Rainbow Medicine Women) is a 6th Generation Shaman with Celtic and Native ancestors.

Her heritage enables her to draw from her roots to connect with the land and its people and the spirits and animals that speak with her.

As, she continues to seek for the truth she helps many interpret their path and purpose and inspires them to seek their own truth.

She continues to hold workshops and ceremonies to facilitate the transformation that is happening on the planet.

Rainbow Medicine Women is a great storyteller, healer and teacher of the Wisdom Teachings.

She resides in the Inner Coastal Mountains of

British Columbia, Canada with her family.

Go to our website for more information on Rainbow's Wellness Camps and Retreats around the world. www.rainbowmedicine.ca

Printed in the United States
By Bookmasters